Also by Deborah Blake

The Little Book of Cat Magic

A Year and a Day of Everyday Witchcraft

Guide to the Everyday Witch Tarot

Everyday Witchcraft

The Witch's Broom

Everyday Witch Book of Rituals

A Witch's Dozen

Everyday Witch A to Z

Witchcraft on a Shoestring

Everyday Witch A to Z Spellbook

The Goddess Is in the Details

Everyday Witch Tarot Coloring Book

Circle, Coven & Grove

Everyday Witch
ORACLE

About the Author

Deborah Blake is the award-winning author of *The Goddess is in the Details*, *Everyday Witchcraft*, and numerous other books from Llewellyn, along with her Everyday Witch Tarot deck. She has published articles in Llewellyn annuals and her ongoing column, "Everyday Witchcraft," is featured in *Witches & Pagans*. She is also the author of the Baba Yaga, Broken Rider, and Veiled Magic series of novels, mostly from Berkley/Penguin.

When not writing, Deborah runs the Artisans' Guild, a cooperative shop she founded with a friend in 1999, and also works as a jewelry maker, tarot reader, and energy healer. She lives in a 130-year-old farmhouse in rural upstate New York with various cats who supervise all her activities, magickal and mundane. She can be found online at Facebook, Twitter, and www.deborahblakeauthor.com.

About the Artist

Elisabeth Alba's fantastical work can be seen in magazines, games, and books, including *Llewellyn's Magical Almanac*. Working traditionally with ink, watercolor, and gouache, Elisabeth was thrilled to delve back into the wondrous world of the Everyday Witch.

After growing up in Pennsylvania and Florida and living in New York City, where she earned a master's degree at the School of Visual Arts, Elisabeth settled in Western Massachusetts with her husband, illustrator Scott Murphy, and dog, Rayo. If she's not lost within a creation on her desk, she's usually found reading, checking out local antique shops and museums, playing board games and puzzles, or traveling. Find her on Instagram, Facebook, Twitter, and www.albaillustration.com.

WISDOM FOR THE
Everyday Witch
ORACLE

Deborah Blake
Art by Elisabeth Alba

LLEWELLYN
WOODBURY MINNESOTA

Everyday Witch Oracle © 2019 by Deborah Blake; art by Elisabeth Alba. All rights reserved. No part of this book may be used or reproduced in any manner whatsoever, including internet usage, without written permission from Llewellyn Publications, except in the case of brief quotations embodied in critical articles and reviews.

First Edition
Fourth Printing, 2021

Cover design by Shannon McKuhen
Editing by Brian R. Erdrich

Llewellyn Publications is a registered trademark of Llewellyn Worldwide Ltd.

ISBN 978-0-7387-5139-9
The Everyday Witch Oracle kit consists of a boxed set of 40 full-color cards and this perfect-bound book.

Llewellyn Worldwide Ltd. does not participate in, endorse, or have any authority or responsibility concerning private business transactions between our authors and the public.

All mail addressed to the author is forwarded but the publisher cannot, unless specifically instructed by the author, give out an address or phone number.

Any internet references contained in this work are current at publication time, but the publisher cannot guarantee that a specific location will continue to be maintained. Please refer to the publisher's website for links to authors' websites and other sources.

Llewellyn Publications
A Division of Llewellyn Worldwide Ltd.
2143 Wooddale Drive
Woodbury, MN 55125-2989
www.llewellyn.com
Printed in China

Contents

INTRODUCTION ... 1

Chapter One:
How to Use this Deck ... 3

Chapter Two:
How the Cards Are Divided ... 9

Chapter Three:
How the Cards Progress ... 11

Chapter Four:
Sample Spreads ... 17

Chapter Five:
The Cards ... 21

Earth: Grounding and Practical Action 21

1. Connect with Gaia 21
2. Hibernation and Regeneration 23
3. Meditation to Dig Deep 24
4. Ground and Center 26
5. Earth Magic 27

6. Plant the Seeds 29

7. Strength and Resilience 31

8. Affirmation for Growth 32

9. Prosperity and Abundance 33

10. Seasonal Harvest 36

Air: **Thought and Communication** 37

1. Imagine and Envision 37

2. Listening to Wisdom 39

3. Meditation for Clarity 40

4. Gratitude and Thanks 42

5. Air Magic 44

6. Learn from Life 46

7. Prayers and Wishes 47

8. Affirmation for Acceptance 49

9. Speak Your Mind 51

10. Transformation and Change 53

Fire: **Creativity and Passion** 55

1. Sun and Stars 55

2. Accept Love 57

3. Meditation for Creativity 59

4. Inspiration and Courage 61

5. Fire Magic 63

6. Give in to Passion 66

7. Follow Your Dreams 68

8. Affirmation for Healing the Heart 69

9. Give Love 71

10. Joy and Delight 73

Water: Change and Movement 76

1. Healing Waters 76

2. Cleansing Body and Spirit 78

3. Meditation for Peace and Serenity 80

4. Change and Progress 82

5. Water Magic 84

6. Make a Move 86

7. Go with the Flow 89

8. Affirmation for Positive Change 90

9. Tears of Joy and Sadness 92

10. Rebirth and Reinvention 94

Chapter Six:
 How to Use this Deck with the Everyday Witch Tarot ... 97

Introduction

Welcome to the Everyday Witch Oracle Deck. Like the Everyday Witch Tarot, also created by author Deborah Blake and illustrator Elisabeth Alba, this deck is intended to be both useful and fun. As the name suggests, there are lots of witches within—both modern and classic, serious and whimsical—often accompanied by cats (but also some dogs, and you never know what else will show up...). And just like the everyday witches you might meet in real life, the witches in this deck come in all sorts of wonderful variations, ready to share their wisdom with all those who want it.

Unlike the tarot, which takes a certain amount of study and practice to really become comfortable with and adept at, the oracle deck can be used as soon as you take the cards out of the box. See—useful and fun already! The cards are divided into suits of ten, and each suit is based on an element: Earth, Air, Fire, or Water. The numbers each have a general theme as well, but neither of those things has to impact your use of the cards unless you choose to focus on them that way.

We purposely set out to make oracle cards that had multiple applications, so they offered a little something for everyone. Unlike the tarot, where the image on the card means something fairly specific, these cards are far simpler. Use them for inspiration, divination, or magic, as the mood strikes you. Let them speak to your own inner wisdom and resonate with your soul.

Or, you know, just pull one every day for fun.

It's completely up to you.

Enjoy!

Chapter One

How to Use this Deck

Let me start by saying that there is no wrong way to use these cards. Oracle cards can be used for everything from inspiration to a call to action, divination, magical work, and more. The only limit is that of your own imagination.

Unlike tarot cards, which have fairly specific meanings (although those meanings will vary from deck to deck and reading to reading), these cards are purposely designed to be more general. This makes them both easier to use and gives them a wider range of applications.

The three most obvious are written out for each individual card in this book, but don't be afraid to come up with your own interpretations or ways of using the deck. Consider this book to be a jumping-off place to your own personal oracle adventure.

For ease of use, each card in this book contains suggestions for three possible approaches: action, divination, and magic. You can either start out with an intention ("Today I'm going to use the oracle cards for divination"), pick a card or cards, and follow that direction, or you can simply pull a card and see which application appeals to you most ("Hey, this action seems like what I should be doing right now").

Oracle cards are most often used as single cards, although there are a few suggestions for simple spreads later in this section. You can shuffle the cards and pick the top one, or spread them out on a table and pick whichever one calls to you. You can even just shuffle them one time and then go down through the deck for the next forty days, seeing what order the cards come up in.

My coven, Blue Moon Circle, often uses oracle cards during ritual to receive messages from the universe/god and goddess or to provide inspiration and guidance. For instance, at Imbolc, we might go around the circle and pull a card to predict what lies ahead for the year to come. At the spring equinox, we may "plant" intentions for the season and pull a card to see what we need to be working on.

I have numerous different oracle decks, some featuring goddesses (we use those to encourage us to look into a goddess we might not already be familiar with) and some with affirmations we can use to lend us strength. There are decks with simple spells, too.

The Everyday Witch Oracle can be used during ritual or you can simply pick up the deck whenever you have a moment of peace and quiet to focus on yourself. Or you can follow the directions in this book, if you are so inclined.

For each card, there will be a general statement, and then suggestions for three different possible approaches. Action for inspiration is just what it sounds like—you can use the card to inspire thought or take an action based on what the card says. Divination—if you are using the deck for divination (much as you would use a tarot deck) then the card you pull has a message for you. The magic option contains a simple and easy magical task for each specific card.

Here's an example of how one card could be used in different ways. This is the information you will find for the "Go with the Flow" card, which is one of the ten cards in the Water suit.

STATEMENT: "Most of us spend a lot of time fighting the challenges and obstacles life puts in our way or pushing back against aspects of our reality we don't like. That's not a bad thing, in and of itself, and many times it is necessary. The trick is in knowing when to fight, and when that resistance is only going to frustrate us and sap our energy, and when to go with the flow instead. Sometimes (to paraphrase some other folks) you just have to give in and give goddess. In short, acknowledge that there is nothing you can do, make your peace with the situation the best you can, and have faith that the gods will make everything work out in the end (even if the way it works out doesn't necessarily make sense to you at the time)."

ACTION: Do something that is easy and fun. Put your problems and concerns aside for the moment and just live, even if it is only for a few hours. Have a relaxed meal with family or friends. Take a dog for a walk (dogs are great at going with the flow). Float in a pool or the ocean or a tub. Take a little space of time to allow yourself to just *be*.

DIVINATION: If there is something in your life that you're using a lot of time, energy, and spirit to fight, this card may be a sign that it is time to stop, at least for a while. Is there a different way of approaching the issue, maybe one that involves compromise or less effort? Can you back away and just let it be for a while? Sometimes going with the flow for a day or two helps you find your way to letting go for good.

MAGIC: Using a source of moving water (a stream or river, rain, or even the water coming from your faucet or some that you pour from a pitcher), picture a goal in your mind and then infuse it into the water. Feel your intentions moving out into the world as the water flows. Then let go and allow the intentions to blossom into fruition if they're going to.

In case you're curious, here is a description of how the picture will look: A female witch sits in a canoe wearing a black hat with her cat perched on the front of the boat. Her paddle can be seen floating away in the current behind the canoe, but she is smiling and at ease despite having no control over where she is going. One hand trails in the water; lovely, plant growth on the shore is abundant; and the sun is shining.

So you could look at the card first to see how it resonates with you, then choose one of the three options to use with it. Or you might know when you start out which approach you want to use. Or, alternatively, you could simply enjoy the card, take in its basic message (who doesn't occasionally need to be reminded to go with the flow?) and then get on with your day.

It is always up to you.

Chapter Two

How the Cards Are Divided

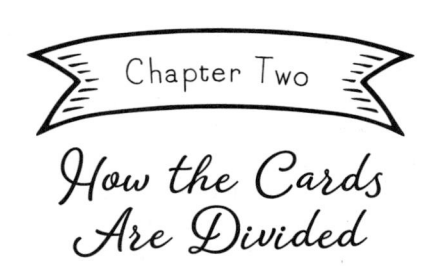

As I mentioned earlier, the forty cards in the deck are divided into groups of four with ten each for Earth, Air, Fire, and Water. Not only are these elements an integral part of a witchcraft practice, but they also surround us in our daily lives. Each different element has its own basic theme and a progression of that theme throughout the ten cards. You can, of course, come up with your own variations on these themes, but here is how I have set them out:

Earth: grounding and practical action
Air: thought and communication
Fire: creativity and passion
Water: change and movement

These themes may not make much of a difference if you are pulling random cards (although if you are pulling a series of cards and they all fall within the same element, the universe may be trying to tell you something!). On the other hand, if there is an area of your life where you feel that you need to focus more attention, you might want to start out by working with the cards that fall under that theme. For instance, if you are feeling stuck, spend some time with the Water cards. If you are having interpersonal issues, maybe try using Air.

Chapter Three

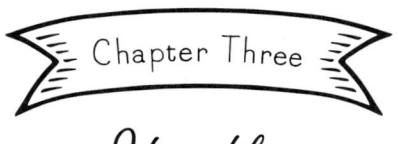

How the Cards Progress

Just as the cards are divided into four different themes, within those themes there is a general pattern. Keep in mind that each time you use the deck, these cards may mean slightly different things, or call to you to approach them in a different manner—one time as inspiration, the next as a magical tool. Alternately, you might find yourself pulling the same card over and over again if that is the message you need to hear or an issue that is still ongoing.

This happens in tarot readings too. I always tell people that if they repeatedly get the same cards, there is probably something they need to change about themselves or their situation in order for the cards to change. This isn't necessarily as true for oracle cards, but it is still a good idea to pay attention if the same card shows up a number of times in a row.

For instance, the number one card is an introduction to the element. This can manifest in various ways, though. So Earth's first card is "Connect with Gaia," Air is "Imagination and Envision," Fire is "Sun and Stars," and Water is "Healing Waters." Each of these cards gives you a way to connect with or embrace the essence of that element.

The number two card in each section is devoted to internal work; it helps you to go inside or be quiet. So the second Earth card is "Hibernation and Regeneration," while Air is "Listening to Wisdom," Fire is "Accept Love," and Water is "Cleansing Body and Spirit." How you use these particular cards is up to you. For instance, the Hibernation and Regeneration card may be a suggestion that you need some time alone, or you could do the magical work associated with that card or divination that is aimed at going deep inside your own intuition.

The number three card is always a meditation card. But this doesn't mean you have to actually meditate (don't panic!). What meditation means in this case is "pay attention." So if you get the Earth card, "Meditation to Dig Deep," that may be a suggestion from the universe that you should be giving some serious thought to something in your life you need to dig into deeper. For Air, you may need a little more clarity. Fire focuses on creativity, and Water guides you toward peace and serenity. Who couldn't use a little more of that? The meditation cards can be used as a springboard to literal meditation, or you can follow the suggested actions in divination or magical practice to explore the cards from those directions.

The number four card focuses on doing the work. It gives you a way to take some aspect of each element and use it as a tool for positive change. In the case of Earth, the four card is "Ground and Center." For this card there will be three different approaches to using the Earth element's gift of grounding. Air, which is all about thought and communication, has a number four card that guides you toward "Gratitude and Thanks." Fire helps you find "Inspiration and Courage," and Water, which is the most fluid of all the elements, is all about "Change and Progress."

The number five card is all about magic. Of course, magic can manifest in many different ways, but this card can help you find the way that is right for you at that particular day and time. Play with the various magical aspects of Earth, Air, Fire, and Water, or simply use the image on the cards to inspire you to find the magic within.

The number six card invites you to take action. For Earth, this means "Plant the Seeds," whether actual or metaphorical. The six card in the Air section is "Learn from Life," which guides you towards not just paying attention to what the universe is trying to teach you, but also to applying that new knowledge in practical ways. Fire's sixth card suggests that you "Give in to Passion," by taking some kind of action on whatever it is you are passionate about, and the Water card tells you to "Make a Move," whether that means exercising your body or your mind.

The number seven cards take further actions, whether that is working on "Strength and Resilience," sending out "Prayers and Wishes," pushing you to "Follow Your Dreams," or just "Go with the Flow." (Sometimes taking *no* action is an action in and of itself, after all.)

Just as the number three card is always a meditation, the number eight card is some form of affirmation. Again, this can be an actual affirmation, or divination or magic that reinforces the positive. The Earth card affirmation centers around "Growth," Air's affirmation is all about "Acceptance," Fire helps with "Healing the Heart," and Water works towards "Positive Change."

The number nine card returns to a focus on action, moving even deeper into a connection with each element. If you are following the card progression through each section instead of randomly, this is where things may really start to fall into place. For Earth, it is all about "Prosperity and Abundance," while Air encourages you to "Speak Your Mind," and Fire suggests that you "Give Love." Water's card is "Tears of Joy and Sadness," but those don't have to be literal tears. There are many ways to work with Water, and this card will help you explore a few of them.

We end with the number ten card—fulfillment. For Earth, this means "Seasonal Harvest," whether actual or symbolic. Air is all about "Transformation and Change," Fire brings us to "Joy and Delight," and Water finishes up with "Rebirth and Reinvention."

All of these themes work whether you are pulling random cards now and again or methodically moving through the entire deck. Just remember that you are free to choose any of the three approaches listed under each card (action, divination, or magic) or simply absorb whatever message the universe is sending you without taking any action at all. There is no right or wrong way to use this deck—simply whatever works best for you.

Chapter Four

Sample Spreads

Most of the time, oracle cards are used individually. You simply pull a card and go with it. But occasionally you may want to ask a question or try a more complicated application. Here are a few basic suggestions for how to use one to three cards.

One Card

- **Guidance:** To get a basic idea of what you need to be looking at, shuffle the deck and pull one card at random.
- **Inspiration:** If you need a card to use as a focus or place on your altar for a while, you can look through the deck and pick out whichever one has the image, symbol, or message you need at the moment.

- **Exploration:** To explore the deck as a whole, or one specific element, work your way through one card at a time.
- **Fun:** Just pull a card, and then do which ever option appeals to you.
- **Divination:** Write down your question, then pull a card at random, either after shuffling the deck or spreading the cards out in a row upside down.
- **Magical work:** Pull a card and use the magic option listed for it. You can do this randomly, or pick a card that seems to apply to whatever you need to work on, or perhaps on the full moon or a Sabbat.

Remember that the cards can be used for any of these purposes during ritual, too, either on your own or with a group.

Two Cards

- **Past and present:** Shuffle the deck and pull one card to represent a past influence and one to represent a current influence. Consider what those things mean in your life and how they might be affecting your actions. Or ask what you need to know about the past and the present as they apply to any particular situation.

- **Two of the same number:** Purposely pick out two cards of the same number from different section. If you pick two of the number four cards, for instance, see if there is a way to use one and then the other for a more powerful experience. For example, if you picked Earth and Fire, you could start with "Ground and Center," and then use what you did with that card to help you work on "Inspiration and Courage."
- **Two with the same general purpose:** If you are working on a particular goal, you might want to use two similar cards. For example, if you want to work on prosperity, you could use the "Plant the Seeds" card and then follow up with "Prosperity and Abundance," whether you choose to do the action, divination, or magical approach.
- **Inspiration:** As with the single card option above, if you need inspiration, you can pull the two cards you find the most meaningful from the deck and either focus on them for a span of time or place them on your altar.
- **Today and tomorrow:** Sit with the cards for a while, maybe shuffling them as you think about what you need to be doing now and what you need to be aiming for, then pull two cards.

Three Cards

- **Past, Present, Future:** This is just like the past and present above, but the third card will represent something you might need to concentrate on for the future. Look at the way the cards work together. Is there a pattern? Does something about the past card have an influence on the present, and what is it about the present card that you need to learn from or overcome to get to the future card?
- **Maiden, Mother, Crone:** In this layout, look for messages from either the three different aspects of the goddess, or perhaps wisdom from your younger self, your current self, and your future self. What are they trying to tell you?
- **Three random cards:** Shuffle the deck and pick three random cards. Maybe they come together with the same message ("Hibernation and Regeneration," "Meditation to Dig Deep," and "Rebirth and Reinvention" might be telling you to take some time to deal with your deeper issues so that you can move on with your life, for instance). Maybe they are three different aspects of your path that would all benefit from some more attention. See if you can see a pattern or if the images on the cards have anything in common.

Chapter Five

The Cards

EARTH: Grounding and Practical Action

1. Connect with Gaia

"The Earth is our Mother, and if we are not in tune with her, the rest of our lives will be out of balance too. The modern world can take us far away from our roots as living, breathing people on a living, breathing planet. Take a few moments to connect with Gaia, whether as the Earth goddess, the ground beneath you, or some growing thing."

ACTION: Go outside and put your feet on the ground. Raise your hands to the sky and feel the connection from above and below. Pull in energy from the earth, and send back a little of your own in gratitude for her gifts. If you can't go outside, plant your feet firmly on the floor wherever you are and feel the energy coming up through the layers between you and the soil that lies beneath you. No matter how high up you are, the earth is down there somewhere.

DIVINATION: Modern life is full of distractions. Make sure you remember to take time to tune in to the earth, no matter what else is going on around you. This card reminds you to stay in touch with what is truly important, both spiritually and practically, especially those things that support the rest of your efforts.

MAGIC: Sit comfortably or stand in front of your altar holding on to the crystal or stone of your choice. Light a candle and concentrate on the stone, sending your awareness deep inside. Try to connect with the energy of the stone; does it feel warm, strong, or comforting? Does this stone have something to offer you that some other stone might not? Does it feel as though it could boost your magical work for prosperity, healing, peace, or any other particular goal?

2. Hibernation and Regeneration

"Sometimes you just need to pull back from the world for a while. Rest, regroup, recharge, so you can return stronger and more capable of dealing with whatever awaits you outside your cave."

ACTION: Take a nap, meditate, or simply curl up someplace quiet with a good book. Take a few minutes to pet a cat or play with a dog. Give yourself a break from pushing forward at full speed without feeling guilty about it. The world is a busy and hectic place, and we all need downtime to give our spirit a little space for its important work behind the scenes.

DIVINATION: This card suggests that you haven't been taking enough time to be quiet and alone. Do you need to take a break from stressful people or situations (or, you know, the internet)? It can be hard to carve out times for ourselves, but burning the candle at both ends just leaves you with a burned-out candle. Even five minutes to breathe can help. You don't have to go into actual hibernation, but you might want to take a walk or sit outside or play in the dirt.

MAGIC: Create a magical cave to retreat into. In front of your altar or in any comfortable spot, light a single candle (either black or white) in an otherwise dim room. Smudge yourself with sage or use a small bowl of salt and water to wash away the cares of the day. Then focus on the candle and visualize yourself inside a safe cave, far from the rest of the world. See it as clearly as you can in your mind's eye, and rest there, feeling protected and calm. Then ask your inner self, "What answers are hiding deep within?" or "What have I been in too big a hurry to pay attention to?" See what thoughts or images come up, without judgment or worry about what they might mean. When you're ready, blow out the candle and emerge back out of the cave.

3. Meditation to Dig Deep

"Our culture often encourages the pursuit of shallow and immediate pleasures, discouraging the deep work that takes time and energy. But sometimes it is important to look more closely, burrow into our own hearts and minds, and discover what lies underneath the surface. Sometimes you have to dig deep to find the truth. You have all the tools to do that; they are just waiting for you to use them. Meditation can help you achieve a deeper connection."

ACTION: Meditate on this statement while focusing on the image on the card. Ask yourself: What areas of my life could benefit from more attention? What am I not looking at deeply enough? What am I afraid I'll see? And how can I put that fear behind me so I can move forward with clear vision?

DIVINATION: This card is telling you to look at some issue more closely. You probably already know which one. This card just reminds you that avoiding a situation won't lead to a solution; instead, you have to dig deep and look for answers…even if you worry that you might not like them. Maybe the universe will surprise you, or maybe it will turn out that looking more deeply with an open mind will lead to answers that aren't obvious on the surface.

MAGIC: In sacred space (either a place you consider sacred or within a ritual circle) prepare a mound of dirt. If you are outside, you can use the dirt in your yard or garden. If you have to be inside, you can use some potting soil in a large bowl. Take a moment to focus on whichever areas of your life you feel need a deeper examination, or questions you have not been able to find the answer to. Then say the following simple spell and start slowly digging into the dirt with your fingers, allowing the wisdom of the earth to flow into you. Say: "Earth so deep and earth so wise, help me see what underneath lies."

4. Ground and Center

"The world is full of distractions that pull us in a million different directions. Sometimes we just need to stop and ground, centering ourselves so that we can stand strong and rooted, no matter what we face. Grounding is good preparation for magical work, but it also helps us if we are facing any challenging situation or even just getting ready to leave the house and deal with daily life."

Action: Do something that grounds you. For some people this is yoga or meditation, for others it is sitting outside under a tree. Figure out what grounds you and then do it. Breathing is always a good place to start, so if you need to ground, take three long, slow breaths and let them out. Remember to feel the strength of the earth below you as you breathe.

Divination: Have you been feeling scattered and frantic? This card is a reminder to ground and center yourself on a regular basis, not just during magical work. Look at the witch on the card—doesn't she look serene? That kind of calm often feels out of reach, but grounding and centering can help move us in that direction.

Magic: Sit or stand on the ground with your feet firmly planted (outside, if you can, but inside will do). Hold a crystal in your hands, in front of your core, near your belly button. Feel the strength of the Earth element that formed it and take that strength into yourself, starting with your core and then moving down through your feet to connect with the ground below. Close your eyes and visualize yourself sending roots down into the ground. Imagine that the gods have left a message for you under the Earth. What does it say? Be sure to thank the element for its gifts.

5. Earth Magic

"Earth magic is at the core of all we do as Pagans and witches and even simply as human beings. The earth supports our feet when we walk, provides the base for the homes that we live in, and springs all life from its fertile soils. We only have one planet, and doing some kind of Earth magic—whether it involves crystals or herbs or even salt—helps remind us of how important the earth is to our magic and to our lives."

ACTION: Take a walk and pay attention to all the growing things around you or plant some seeds in a garden or a container inside. There is a certain magic in starting new life in the soil and watching it grow and blossom. For something even more practical, do something good for the earth like planting a tree, cleaning up litter, or creating a welcoming space in your yard for birds or critters. As you do any of these things, be mindful of your connection to the element of Earth and fill your heart with gratitude for her gifts.

DIVINATION: This card is telling you to do something magical! Magic means something different to each of us, but pick an action that seems magical to you that will connect you to the element of Earth and do it today. It doesn't have to be a long complicated ritual (although that's not a bad idea either). Magic feeds the soul as the earth nourishes our bodies. Do something magical. Your spirit will thank you.

MAGIC: Take a walk and pick up the first rock that catches your eye. See if you can perceive any shapes or symbols in or on it. If you have rocks or crystals at home, you can use one of them. Crystals in particular often have inclusions or internal fractures that change in appearance every time you look at them.

6. Plant the Seeds

"All things that grow have to start somewhere, with seeds both actual and metaphorical. Whether it is the seed of an idea, a new beginning, or a garden of magical herbs, you have to plant it, and then nurture it well to get the results you want. Caring for your seeds takes effort, but sometimes the biggest challenge is having the courage and forward momentum to plant them at all. What seeds are you planting in your life?"

ACTION: Plant a seed. Heck, plant a dozen; they're small. Do you like flowers? Then plant flower seeds. Like to cook? Plant culinary herbs or a simple vegetable like lettuce or spinach. They grow fast and give you nearly instant gratification. Want something magical? Plant the seeds for magical herbs or (if you live where it is warm and dry) even the white sage used in sage smudge sticks. Or, of course, you could start on a new project. That counts too. Plant the seeds for anything that will grow over time and bring you joy.

DIVINATION: This card probably isn't telling you to plant an actual seed. Instead, it suggests that it is time to start something new. Is it time to look for a new job, embark on an adventure, or encourage a budding relationship? Plant the seeds for future growth in your life, even if you have to start small. Is there some project you have been considering? This card is a hint that it might be time to take the first step.

MAGIC: Most witches use herbs and other plants in their magical work. Growing them yourself gives you a chance to put your energy and your intentions into them from the very beginning, which makes them even more powerful. Chose an herb that is easy to grow (most of the common ones are) and prepare some soil in your garden if you have one, or in a pot inside if you don't. Press the seeds firmly into the soil while saying, "Element of Earth, receive these seeds which I dedicate to positive magical work. Nourish them and strengthen them, and bless them with your power. So mote it be." Don't forget to tend them with extra special care afterwards and thank the plant when you clip a bit for magical work later.

7. Strength and Resilience

"Strength means different things at different points of our lives. Sometimes it means having the physical strength to run marathons, climb mountains, or dance until the wee hours of the morning. Sometimes it means having the emotional strength to triumph over adversity. We can't all be Superman and leap tall buildings in a single bound, but we can be strong in the ways that are important. Sometimes strength is less about muscles and more about will."

ACTION: Do something that challenges you, something that calls on just a little more strength than you think you have. Walk a little farther than usual. Stand up to a bully. Give up an addiction. Be strong. You can do it.

DIVINATION: This card is telling you one of two things—or maybe both. If you wanted to know if you should or could do something, the answer is: "Yes, go for it. You have the strength and ability to succeed." If you just pulled a card for general information or inspiration, then this card is telling you that you are stronger than you think. Take heart.

Magic: To do a simple spell for strength and courage, light an orange, white, or brown candle. Focus on what strength means to you and pull on the strength of the earth below. Visualize yourself growing strong roots and a trunk like a mighty tree. Feel your limbs stretch up toward the sky and say, "Earth, lend me your strengths, so that I am strong like the oak, able to stand against the storms of life."

8. Affirmation for Growth

"Growth is necessary for life. The opposite of growth is stagnation, and no one wants to be stuck, sitting still, and never moving forward. Growth takes effort, and sometimes it can be scary. It doesn't happen by itself—you have to nurture and feed it, whether it is body, spirit, or some part of your life, like a career or a relationship. What do you want to grow and prosper in your life? And what are you doing to make that happen?"

Action: Take an action that will help some aspect of your life to grow in a positive way. Or reach out and help someone else to grow, like a child who needs guidance or a friend who could use a helping hand. Do something to nurture the earth or tend a garden (whether it is outside or inside on a windowsill).

Divination: This card is telling you it is time to stop standing still. Is there a project you have been working on? You might want to give it more energy and attention. Or take a look at your life and see if it is moving forward in the ways you would like it to. If not, what can you do to change that? Are your relationships growing and blooming? How can you nurture them so they do? This card reminds you that all growth must be nurtured and encouraged.

Magic: Write down a list of the things you want to grow in your life. Put it in the bottom of a small pot and put some soil on top of it. Then put in a few seeds (or a small plant, if you aren't good at starting things from scratch) and hold it in your hands for a few minutes. Think about what you can do to help with that growth—concrete, practical actions—and vow to yourself that you will follow through on doing them. Send that intention out into the universe. When you're done, put the pot on your altar or some other safe place where you will see it often and remember your commitment to growth.

9. Prosperity and Abundance

"Prosperity and abundance are not exactly the same things, and they may mean something different to each of us. Prosperity usually has to do with monetary success, but it can also mean the feeling of success and good fortune, which you can have even without money. Abundance means having enough of what you need, plus maybe a little bit more. Feeling as though you have prosperity and abundance is less about how much money you have than how you view your life. Remember to count your blessings instead of just the coins in your wallet."

ACTION: It is easy to look at life from the position of "lack." There are always things we want, or even need, that we don't have. But for most of us, the reality is that we are still better off than many others. Take a piece of paper and draw a line down the middle. On one side, write down the things you don't have that you wish you did. Maybe that's a new car, or a better job, a nicer place to live, or even a new book by a favorite author. On the other side, write down the things you have—a roof over your head, food on the table, people who love you. No matter how large or how small, write down the good things in your life. Look at both sides of the list. Does one greatly outnumber the other? Now take another look at your "want" side of the list, and draw a line through anything you really don't need. (It's okay to want things, but it's good to be aware that there is a difference between want and need.) Now look at your lists again; I'll bet they will surprise you.

DIVINATION: This card is a suggestion that you count your blessings. The universe is telling you that you have whatever you need and probably much of what you want. If you're asking about a project or goal of some kind, the answer is almost certainly yes; it will be a success. But mostly, it is a symbol of what you already have and a reminder to appreciate it.

MAGIC: Here is a simple bit of prosperity magic. Take a coin (it is fun to use a special one, like a dollar or half-dollar coin, but any kind will do, even a simple copper penny) and hold it in your hands. Close your eyes and think about what form you would like prosperity to come to you in—actual money, a gift, a specific need fulfilled, a new job, whatever—and send that desire out into the universe and also down into the coin. Then take the coin and bury it in the dirt. You can use a small pot filled with soil, shove it into a planter inside, or put it out in your garden if you have one. Give the soil a little pat to say thank you, then go do whatever you can to make your wishes for prosperity come true, knowing that you have given them a magical boost.

10. Seasonal Harvest

"With hard work, and a little dollop of luck, our endeavors will eventually bear fruit. No matter what form this takes for you, be sure to take the time to celebrate the harvest. Whether it is an actual harvest of food from your garden or a metaphorical harvest of something you have been working toward, it is important to stop, take a breath, and feel the joy and gratitude that comes with any achievement that took time and effort."

ACTION: Life is full of disappointments and setbacks, no matter how hard you work. This makes it even more important to celebrate the victories, both large and small. Find something you succeeded at recently (even if it is just surviving a tough day at work) and reward yourself with a small celebration, whether it is a favorite food, a soak in the tub, or doing something fun with friends. Go, you!

DIVINATION: This card may be an indication that it is time to finish off a project, complete a task you have been working on, or do whatever it takes for you to finally reap the rewards of your hard work. Alternatively, it might be telling you that the harvest is done and celebration is in order. Hurrah!

MAGIC: There is magic in food, especially when it is fresh and healthy. Treat yourself to a feast (even if it is a little one, like a bowl of berries) either by yourself or with friends. Find the freshest fruits and veggies you can and ask the gods to bless them before you eat them. Give thanks to the earth that nurtured them and eat mindfully, aware that you are taking in the power and strength of the Earth element with every bite.

AIR: Thought and Communication

1. Imagine and Envision

"Imagination is at the core of any witchcraft practice. After all, if you are working toward some sort of goal, you have to be able to imagine it first. And unless you are lucky enough to be visited by an actual manifestation of god and goddess, you probably have to come up with an image that represents them to you. We use imagination and visualization all the time—in prayer and ritual, spellcasting, and meditation. And just like any other skill, using your imagination becomes easier with practice. So let your imagination soar, today and every day."

ACTION: There are a million different ways to use your imagination. Make up a story (for yourself, or to tell to kids), draw, paint, or even just daydream. Think about which magical creatures you'd like to meet and what they might be like if you did. Picture yourself as a pirate, a princess, a wizard. Even if it is just for five minutes a day as you are falling asleep, imagine wild and wonderful things. Or simply imagine five minutes of peace, sitting by the shore of the ocean. That counts too.

DIVINATION: This card reminds you to use your imagination. Are you limiting the solutions to a problem because you can't imagine possibilities beyond the obvious? Maybe you are feeling discouraged and need to dream big about your future. Let your imagination roam and see what comes up. Then pay attention.

MAGIC: Imagination is a vital magical tool. To practice using it, pick a goal—it can be prosperity or love or peace or healing, whatever you chose to concentrate on today. Light a yellow candle (white will do) and stare into the flame. Imagine you can see images in the flickering light or close your eyes and visualize the images that way. Imagine things that could lead to your goal. For instance, if you are working on healing, you might imagine a bright healing light surrounding your body. Make those images as vivid and real as you can.

2. Listening to Wisdom

"We spend a lot of time surrounding ourselves with noise—television, phones, even our own voices. It can be hard to hear anything above the constant hum and buzz of everyday life. But sometimes you have to take time to be quiet and listen. Really listen. Maybe the universe or the gods have been trying to tell you something and you haven't been able to hear it. Maybe it is your own inner wisdom that is crying out to be heard. How will you know if you don't take the time to listen?"

ACTION: Go someplace where you can be quiet. If you are staying in your own house, turn off the phone, the TV, anything that makes noise. If it helps, you can dim the lights as well or go outside after dark and sit under the moon. Or sit by a body of water, if there is one nearby. Then just…sit. Don't do anything. Quiet your mind as much as you can, and ask, "Is there anything I need to know?" Then listen to see if you get an answer from without or within.

Divination: This card is telling you you're missing something. Whether it is someone close to you, the gods, or just your own inner wisdom trying to tell you something important (with or without putting it into words), it is time to SHUT UP AND LISTEN.

Magic: If there is a message you are supposed to be receiving, sometimes a little magical work can help to make it clearer. Follow the "action" instructions above, but cast a magical circle before you settle in so that you are doing your listening in sacred space. Maybe light a candle or smudge yourself with sage to waft away the cares of your everyday life that might be distracting you from truly listening. Then ask the power of Air to help send you the information you need to know. Open a window if you can and see if the wind will whisper to you.

3. Meditation for Clarity

"It can be hard for us to see things clearly, and the closer we are to them, the harder it can be. This is especially true when we are looking at ourselves or at the important issues that affect our lives. When strong emotion is involved, that makes it even tougher. But that doesn't mean it is impossible—just that we have to make a special effort to reach for clarity."

ACTION: Meditate on this statement while focusing on the picture on the card. Ask yourself, "Do I see myself with clear and honest eyes? What about the people and situations around me? Is there something I know in my heart I need to look at more clearly?" Try to put aside emotion for a moment and simply be, then look again.

DIVINATION: This card is a suggestion that it is time to seek out clarification of an issue or issues or to look more closely at something that perhaps you have been viewing through eyes clouded with emotion or the prejudicial statements of others. Do not take things at surface value, but rather make sure that what you think you are seeing is really the truth.

MAGIC: Take a dark bowl and fill it with water. Light a candle and place it so that it reflects upon the surface of the water and then smudge yourself and the water with a sage wand. As the smoke from the sage drifts away, say, "Great gods, please help me to see with clarity of vision and an open heart." Then stare into the water and see if anything appears to you, either in the water or in your mind's eye. (You can concentrate on a particular question or situation if you have one in mind.)

4. Gratitude and Thanks

"It is easy to take the good things for granted, especially at times when the bad stuff is overwhelming. But those are the moments when it is the most important to pause and give thanks for what you *do* have, instead of dwelling on what you don't. If you are dealing with a health issue, focus on the parts of your body that work correctly or thank the ones with issues for doing the best they can under the circumstances. Don't have enough money? Be grateful for what you do have. And especially give thanks to the people who are there for you, in both good times and bad. Scientific studies have proven that an attitude of gratitude is actually healthy. But you already knew that, didn't you? Sometimes we all just need a little reminder to be grateful and say thank you."

ACTION: What are you grateful for? Spend five minutes a day—maybe when you first wake up or right before you fall asleep—listing all the things in your life you are thankful for, including all the people. They don't have to be big things—a purring cat, a beautiful sunset, enough food to eat, someone letting you cut ahead in the checkout line...anything that made your life even the tiniest bit better. Do this for a week and see if you feel better or at least more aware of how much good there is in your life.

DIVINATION: If you pull this card, it is probably a reminder to say thank you. Thank you to the gods, to the universe, the people in your life, even to yourself for all your hard work (and just for getting out of bed in the morning on the days when that seems nearly impossible). Ask yourself if you have been cultivating an attitude of gratitude or if, instead, you have been focusing on the negative and forgetting to be grateful for all that is positive.

MAGIC: Place a number of small tea lights on a fire-safe plate. Light a candle in the darkness (or a bonfire, if you can do that) and take a moment to feel your heart fill with gratitude for the many things that bring light into your life. Invite in any god or goddess you follow (or deity in general) to witness your gratitude and appreciation for their gifts. Light a tea light and say thank you for something specific. Repeat with as many tea lights as you wish.

Concentrate on your intention to send that feeling of gratitude out into the universe as strongly as you can. Then put both hands over your heart and thank yourself for being present and aware. If you like, finish up by saying, "I thank god and goddess for the many blessings in my life and ask them to help me continue to be mindful and appreciative. So mote it be."

5. Air Magic

"Without air there is no life. But unlike the Earth element, which is solid and obvious, the element of Air is more ephemeral and harder to visualize. You cannot, after all, hold a chunk of air in your hands, the way you can a rock. So we often use something else to symbolize it, like a feather, or incense. But that doesn't make it any less vital an element than Earth—or any less powerful, as anyone who has ever lived through a hurricane will tell you. Embrace the power of Air with every breath and send your appreciation out on the breeze."

ACTION: There is a simple way to connect with the magic of Air, and you do it all the time—breathing. But instead of breathing without conscious effort, take a few moments to sit and really be aware of the air moving in and out of your lungs. Feel the power you draw in with every breath and the cleansing that carries away what you don't need as you exhale. If you want, visualize the breath coming in as one color (yellow, for instance) and the breath going out as another (gray, as it wafts away negativity). Be sure to say thank you to the element for its gifts.

DIVINATION: This card is telling you to do something magical connected to Air! You can do the breathing exercise above or stand outside in the wind as you mindfully connect to the power of Air. If you have been struggling with health or emotional issues, light a sage smudge stick and let the air waft away negativity and illness.

MAGIC: To make a magical connection with Air, light a white or yellow candle. If you like, you can place a feather in front of it to symbolize the element. Then light either incense or a sage smudge stick and blow on it (or if you can be outside, let the breeze do the job for you). Watch the patterns the smoke makes as it rises. Can you see anything in the smoke the way you see shapes in the clouds? Let the smoke waft around you, magically connecting you to the element.

6. Learn from Life

"Someone once said that those who do not learn from their mistakes are doomed to repeat them. Have you been learning as you move through life or are you still doing the same thing over and over again and wondering why your situation hasn't changed? There are many different ways to learn—books, experience, the wisdom of others. But if you want to become your own best self, it is important to keep learning from life's lessons, large and small. What have you learned today?"

ACTION: Make an effort to learn something new today. You can try something different and see what happens, do some research, or read a bit in a book by one of your favorite authors. Or you could talk to someone who has had experiences you haven't and ask them about it. (Hint: Older people may know a *lot* of things you don't! Maybe talk to a parent, grandparent, community elder, or neighbor, and ask them what they've learned in their travels.)

DIVINATION: This card suggests that maybe you need to be paying more attention to the lessons the universe is sending you. Is there something you should be doing differently but aren't because you haven't learned from your mistakes? Or is there some way you could be improving your life if only you were willing to expand your knowledge? Make sure that you are embracing life and experiencing it fully.

MAGIC: Sometimes we need help figuring out what the lesson is that we are supposed to be taking away from a particular situation or challenge (especially if strong emotions are involved). Sit in front of a yellow or white candle. If you want, you can put a book next to the candle to symbolize knowledge. Light the candle and say, "God and goddess, please help me to learn from life as fully and gracefully as possible."

7. Prayers and Wishes

"A spell is much like a prayer—it is a way to send your hopes and thoughts and wishes and worries out into the universe, to gain the attention of a deity with the power to help. Sometimes prayers are just general wishes: 'Please make this better. I wish I had more money. If only I could find love.' Sometimes they are addressed to a particular god or goddess, or to the universal powers that be. No matter how you look at them, we all have moments when, no matter what form they take, we need to put out a prayer or a wish and hope for an answer."

ACTION: Think about what you really need or want in your life. Not the little things but the stuff that is really important to you. Then, as many of us did when we were children, wait for the first star to rise in the night sky and send your wish out with all your energy, saying, "Star light, star bright; first star I see tonight. Wish I may, wish I might, have the wish I wish tonight."

DIVINATION: If you get this card, it may be telling you it is time to ask for help from a greater source. Or perhaps it is a hint that you should put more energy behind the prayers and wishes that really matter to you and start working on making those wishes come true.

MAGIC: If a spell is a kind of prayer, then putting your prayers and wishes into a spell is the perfect way to go. Figure out what you really want to ask for, and write it down on a piece of paper. Bless the prayer with the power of Air by waving a feather over it or wafting it with incense or sage. Then say, "I pray for dreams and wishes true, for help from the gods above. I ask these wishes old and new, with perfect trust and love." Hold the paper in your hands and put all the energy from your prayers into it, and then make it into the shape of a paper airplane and send it sailing out into the world. (If you can't do that, you can sail the airplane to your altar or some other safe place.)

8. Affirmation for Acceptance

"There is a prayer that says, 'God grant me the serenity to accept the things I cannot change.' Sometimes, no matter how hard we try, there are circumstances or realities that we can't alter. Illnesses, broken relationships, lost jobs…there are, unfortunately, plenty of things in our lives we can't fix. It can be difficult not to keep fighting, but sometimes battling the unchangeable just uses up time and energy that would be better used in more productive ways. Sometimes what we really need is simply the serenity to accept those things we cannot change and the wisdom to know when it is time to do so."

ACTION: For a practical exercise, make a list. On one side, list the things that you don't like about your life that you have some control over and make some concrete plans for how to change them. On the other side, list the things about your life that make you unhappy and that you have no control over whatsoever. Give some thought to how much of your energy is going toward being angry and frustrated about those things and how much time you spend fighting the impossible or just plain complaining. Once you've contemplated it for a while, take that half of the list and rip it into shreds. Then let the tiny pieces of paper go the next time there is a strong wind.

DIVINATION: This card is probably trying to tell you that there is something you need to simply accept. You almost certainly know what it is already. You just needed a nudge to let go and let goddess. Whatever it is, be kind to yourself and stop fighting. Take a deep breath, admit that there are some battles you can't win, and move on.

MAGIC: Sometimes it can be tough to accept that fate or the gods might have plans that are different than the ones you had. It's okay to ask for help. Here is a simple prayer for acceptance and peace. Dab a little lavender essential oil on a white candle or rub some of the herb (dried or fresh) between your palms. Let the power of Air carry the healing, calming scent inside you, and breath slowly and deeply. Light the candle and say, "God and goddess, please give me the strength to accept the things I cannot change. Help me to be strong enough to let go and wise enough to know when it is time to do so. Let me make peace with the parts of my life that are outside of my control and guide me so I might use my energy wisely. Give me peace and serenity. So mote it be." Then sit and breath for a while. If you are struggling with acceptance, carry a small lavender sachet or dab a bit of essential oil on your clothing or a tissue tucked into your pocket, so the aroma will remind you of this spell.

9. Speak Your Mind

"The element of Air rules over speech, probably because our words are carried on our breath. (Go ahead—try holding your breath and speaking at the same time.) Many of us have a hard time saying what is really on our minds. We either hold back from speaking because of insecurity or fear of causing a fuss, or we speak *too* freely or clumsily, never quite managing to say what we want to the way we want it to come out. Open, honest communication is *hard*. But it is also the cornerstone of all good relationships, whether personal or professional, so it is worth making the effort to get it right, no matter how difficult that might be."

Action: If you have trouble speaking your mind, try practicing in the mirror or with a friend you trust. If you are going into a difficult situation where you will need to be speaking, ask the element of Air to lend you its power and feel that power with every breath you take.

Divination: If you pull this card, the universe is probably telling you that you need to speak up. Is there an issue or situation that you have been struggling with, maybe keeping silent when you had something important to say? Do you feel as though you are not being heard at work or in your personal relationships? Remember that you can speak your mind politely and assertively without being nasty or argumentative. If you get to speak your mind, that means you have to listen too. But don't let anyone or anything rob you of your own voice.

Magic: Sometimes it takes extra courage to be able to speak up when it is easier or safer to remain silent. If you need a boost, call on Mercury, the Roman god of eloquence and communication. Mercury carried a staff known as the caduceus, which is a stick with two snakes wound around it, sometimes topped by a pair of wings. If you are going into a situation where you need to be able to speak your mind with strength and conviction, draw (or download and print out) a picture of a caduceus and write your name across it. Ask Mercury to bless the staff and your voice and carry the picture with you when you need it.

10. Transformation and Change

"There is no growth without change. But change can be scary. It means opening up to something new and different, and often involves taking a risk, something many of us aren't all that comfortable doing. But all of life is about transformation. We are born as babies, grow to be toddlers, then teens, until we transform into adults. Eventually, if we are lucky, we will continue to transform, from young into old, from foolish into wise, from newbie witches into wise old crones and sages. Life is all about transforming ourselves; re creating who we are as we grow and learn and move from who we once were into who we are going to be. You can fight it or you can embrace it, but transformation is going to happen. Isn't it better to willingly become a butterfly than to struggle to stay a chrysalis forever?"

ACTION: Take some time to think about where you are in your life right now and where you want to end up. What transformations need to happen along the way for you to reach your goals and what are you doing to encourage and support those transformations? What do you need to do differently?

DIVINATION: This card is either a confirmation that you are on the right path to successful transformation (in which case, be sure to give yourself a huge huzzah and appreciate all the hard work you've put in) or a suggestion that you need to be looking more closely at what you need to do to get there. You will almost certainly know which one. If you have just completed a major task or transition, take time to celebrate your accomplishments before you move on to the next phase of growth and change.

MAGIC: To smooth the progress of transition, sometimes it is necessary to let go of old patterns or situations that no longer work for you. Just like a butterfly crawling out of a chrysalis, there are parts of where you came from that have to be discarded and left behind in order to move on to new ways of being. If you want to do magical work to help with this process, go outside (especially if there is a breeze or wind) or sit inside in front of an open window, a small fan, or anything else that will blow air on you. (If you can't do either of those things, then move around, dancing or jumping, to cause the air to move around you.) Light a sage smudge stick and let the air waft around and past you. Visualize whatever it is that you need to let go of being blown away with the air and the smoke.

FIRE: Creativity and Passion
1. Sun and Stars

"Fire is one of the easiest of the elements to tune in to. Not just because you can simply light a candle (although there is that), but also because fire exists all around us, all the time. After all, the sun is at its heart a big ball of fire. So are the stars, although they are so distant we can't feel their warmth. So don't worry if you don't have space for a bonfire, or the time to sit and watch a candle burn. Simply turn your face to the sun or look up at the stars and remember that the element of Fire is in more places than you think."

ACTION: Do something to connect with the element of Fire. Light a candle or go out and stand underneath the sun or stars (if it is warm and not raining!). Think about all the aspects of modern life that would never have existed if humans hadn't discovered fire. If it is cold, appreciate the warmth that fire brings us. If it is dark, consider what it would be like to live without the light. Thank the fire for all its gifts, then go turn on your stove and make something yummy, fire up the BBQ, or roast a marshmallow!

DIVINATION: This card is a reminder to expand the way you connect to the elements, in this case, Fire in particular. Do you use the same symbols to represent it in every ritual you do? Maybe it is time to switch things up. Do you take it for granted in your life? Perhaps you need to make an effort to be more mindful of the role it plays not just in witchcraft but in day-to-day survival. Fire is a powerful ally. Don't forget to appreciate it in all its aspects.

MAGIC: Do this simple ritual to connect with the element of Fire. Stand outside during a sunny day or inside in a patch of sun (if you have a cat, you can probably follow it to find one). Close your eyes and feel the warmth on your face. Wait until it gets just a bit uncomfortable—too bright, too hot—and you can truly understand the power of Fire in its simplest and most basic form. Then say, "I greet you, O element of Fire, and respectfully thank you for your presence in my life. Thank you for your light and for your warmth and for the passion you bring to all things. So mote it be."

2. Accept Love

"For many of us, it is easy to give love to others. It may be a little more difficult to accept it in return. Accepting love means believing that you are worthy of the gift, and not all of us really believe that we are. Accepting love can also feel risky; after all, if you open yourself to love, it can then be taken away, leaving yourself feeling vulnerable and hurt. Passion, like fire, can burn us. But it is still worth it. Only in both the giving and receiving of love can we form balanced relationships, whether between friends, family, or romantic partners. You don't have to let people in if their affection seems false or comes with a price. But if those around you offer love freely and genuinely, try to accept it with an open heart. I assure you, you *do* deserve it."

ACTION: Sit someplace quiet and light a red or pink candle. (White will always do as a substitute.) Gaze at the flame for a few minutes, breathing deeply. Feel your heart open and expand. As you exhale, send love out to all those you care for deeply. As you inhale, take in the love that others have offered you. If you aren't feeling that at the moment, then take in the love of the goddess, who is always there and always ready to give it. Repeat as needed when you are feeling alone or having trouble letting love in.

Divination: This card may be a not-so-subtle hint that you need to work on accepting love from others. Have you been feeling unworthy or shutting yourself off from those who want to share genuine affection? Are you more comfortable giving than receiving? (Or perhaps, not doing either?) Keep in mind that you can accept love without giving any promises for the future, if that love is given freely and without strings. If this is something you struggle with, try saying this affirmation, "I am a child of the goddess and I am worthy of being loved." Alternatively, this card could be an indication that someone close to you—a friend, a family member, or even a pet—is struggling to learn how to let love in. If that is the case, don't give up on them.

Magic: The heart chakra is, as its name suggests, the one that rules giving and receiving love. If your heart chakra is blocked or out of balance, that can make it difficult to do either. Sit with your hands over the center of your chest and close your eyes. If you like, you can visualize this chakra either as pink, or a combination of pink and green. Try to sense whether or not energy is flowing smoothly up toward the throat chakra above and down toward your core. In your mind's eye, try moving the energy in your heart chakra clockwise. If it won't spin in that direction, try spinning it in reverse, counterclockwise. Usually, if you really focus, you can get the colored energy to move first in one direction, then the other. If it seems to be stuck (or if you see gray or black overwhelming the pink), try visualizing the healing warmth of the element of Fire melting away any blockages, and surround your heart with light. Send yourself love. That is always a good place to start.

3. Meditation for Creativity

"Creativity can be thought of as the Fire of the spirit. It comes to each of us in different forms. Some people might enjoy creativity in the more obvious artistic directions, such as writing, painting, or crafting. Others might excel at creative problem solving or making their surroundings look beautiful. You can create in an art studio or in a kitchen or even in an office. The only limits are the ones we put on ourselves. Not everyone has the inclination or talent to do everything, but we all have something we make with a combination of mind, heart, hands and spirit. If you haven't figured out what your creative gift is, go out and discover it today."

ACTION: Do something creative. It doesn't matter what. Write a poem or a spell. (Don't worry, they don't have to rhyme.) Paint a picture, throw a pot, or knit something. Whip up something wonderful in the kitchen or rearrange a room so that it feels more peaceful or looks more beautiful. Don't tell yourself you don't have time or talent. Just do it. But more than that—do it with purpose, mindfully, and with appreciation. Really *feel* the creative process and how it nurtures your spirit and keeps your inner fires burning.

DIVINATION: If you have been feeling stagnant or grumpy, maybe this card is trying to tell you that you aren't devoting enough time and energy to the creative part of your nature. After all, work is important, but we all need to balance it out with moments of play. Take a moment to look at this card and ask yourself, "What am I doing to feed my soul?"

MAGIC: Light a red, orange, or white candle and invoke the goddess Brigid. She is a Celtic goddess of creativity and inspiration. She is also known as the goddess of the flame and the well and rules over the cauldron of creativity. If you have a small cast-iron cauldron, you can use that, otherwise any pottery bowl will do. Take scraps of paper and write down any creative forms of expression that interest you. (You don't have to be good at them—these are just things you enjoy doing.) Put the papers in your cauldron or bowl and mix them up with your finger or an athame. Then ask Brigid to guide you and pull out a slip. Set aside time to do whatever is on it, even if it is just an hour or less. If you like, you can put the cauldron or bowl on your altar and pull a different piece of paper every week.

4. Inspiration and Courage

"Life is full of challenges. Some of them we take on willingly. Some of them come out of nowhere when we least expect them. Good or bad, happy or sad, all those things that challenge us also give us the opportunity to grow stronger, to push our boundaries and move out of our comfort zones, to reach deep inside or reach out toward others. Whether you are seeking inspiration for work or play or dealing with illness or grief, don't underestimate the power of your own thoughts."

ACTION: We all have patterns of thinking that are a part of who we are as human beings. Some of them work for us. Some don't. During a challenging time, or when you are seeking to push yourself to be more creative or make big changes, it is easy for those old patterns of thought to get in the way of forward movement. Take a few minutes to consider your own patterns: do you default to the positive or the negative? (Is your glass half empty or half full?) Do you automatically think, "I can do it" or "I'll never succeed"? Are you willing to try new things or do you cling to the old, even when you know it isn't working? Do you let other people help you if you need help or believe you must always tough things out on your own? If everything is working perfectly, that's great. But if not, perhaps it is time to consider changing those patterns. It's hard work, but it can be done if you stay self-aware and keep plugging away at it.

DIVINATION: If you get this card, you are probably in need of either inspiration or courage, or possibly both. That's okay, because this card is also telling you it is out there. Or maybe waiting right inside you. If it is inspiration you need, look to the natural world that surrounds you. It is full of wonders. But don't forget to look inside, too. The human mind is an amazing place, filled with ideas and possibilities that few of us explore fully. If courage is what you seek, you may discover you have a core of inner strength you never knew existed. But don't forget to allow others to encourage you and to reach out to the god and goddess and the elemental forces of the universe; spiritual beliefs, no matter what they are, can be a great source of both inspiration and courage if you remember to call on them when you need them.

MAGIC: Carnelian is a wonderful stone for both creativity and courage. Find a carnelian crystal or tumbled rock or even a piece of jewelry with carnelian in it, if you want to have it with you often. Sit with it for a while in front of your altar or someplace quiet outside and ask the element of Fire to help you connect to the power inside the stone. Ask for help with whatever you need and feel the stone vibrate with that power. Then either carry it with you or hold on to it when you need that extra boost.

5. Fire Magic

"Who hasn't been enchanted by the soft glow of candlelight or the cheerful dancing flames of a bonfire? Fire magic is all around us and is perhaps the easiest to integrate into our everyday lives with a touch of kitchen witchery. The element of Fire is all about creativity and passion and energy, but just like fire itself, too much of any of these things can burn us up and burn us out. On the other hand, if you are feeling as though your own internal flames are burning low, perhaps you need to add a little Fire magic into your life."

ACTION: The simplest way to connect to the magic of Fire is to light a candle. This can be anything from the smallest tea light on your altar to a set of beautiful beeswax tapers added to your dinner table. Light a candle and send out a prayer or just sit in meditation for five minutes as you watch the flame. Commit to lighting a candle (the same one, briefly, or a series of candles that you let burn down until they are gone) every night for a month, and see if you don't feel a little bit more in tune with the power of Fire. But don't forget to use firesafe containers and don't leave lit candles unattended, especially around small children or pets. You don't want that power to go up in flames!

DIVINATION: This card has an obvious message—time to connect with the magical aspects of Fire! If you have a place to do so, light a bonfire and dance around it in celebration of this powerful element. If you can't do that, light a candle (or a bunch of candles) or stir up a pot of something magical on the stove. Add some spices for some extra heat!

MAGIC: Take Fire magic to the next level by adding some special magical touches to a basic candle. Using a pillar or votive candle, use a sharp point (the tip of your athame, a toothpick, or even the tip of a crystal) to etch symbols into the wax. These symbols can vary, depending on what you are trying to achieve with your spell work. For instance, if you are working toward prosperity, you can use rune symbols like Gifu or Fehu, a dollar sign, or anything else that represents your goal. If you are working on love, you might etch a heart (or two) onto your candle. Then anoint the candle with magical oil or an essential oil that is suited to your task (lavender for healing, for example). If you really want to go over the top, you can make your own candle from scratch and add herbs into the wax. Just remember during all that you do to concentrate on the power of Fire and to draw on that when you finally light your extra magical candle.

6. Give in to Passion

"There are times in life when the best thing you can do is to give in to passion. Whether it is the fire of a new relationship, the excitement of creating art, or simply the joy of spending a day on the beach under the heat of the sun, it can be good to let yourself go and just *be*. As long as whatever you are passionate about is a positive force in your life—love, or creativity, or just plain fun—it is important to occasionally stop worrying about being practical and simply follow your bliss."

ACTION: Do something today that gives you that burst of energy and satisfaction. It doesn't matter what it is as long as you are doing something that sparks that fire in your spirit. If you love to cook or bake, do that. (And then share it with your friends or family.) If you are a creative person, work on your art, writing, or whatever it is that you get the most pleasure out of creating. Does helping other people bring you that feeling? How about digging in the dirt in your garden or flower bed? Do that. Even if only for an hour. Half an hour, if that's all you have to spend. Or, you know, there's always sex. That counts as passion too, as long as you're doing it with the right person for the right reasons.

Light a fire in your body, mind, and soul, and revel in the gifts of the element of Fire.

DIVINATION: This card is probably telling you that you are working too hard and playing too little. Are you putting aside enough time to do the things that you are passionate about? Have you even allowed yourself to consider what those things might be? If the answer to either or both of those questions is no, you may want to consider giving in to passion. Remember that we all draw energy from the well of our spirit; if you don't occasionally do something to replenish that well, sooner or later you will come up empty. It may seem frivolous to spend time doing things you love just because you love them, but life can't be only about doing what is necessary and practical. Leave space for the passions of the heart, make time for the people and activities that bring you joy and all the other aspects of your life will benefit.

MAGIC: Light a red candle. Look at the card and see the image of the witch being carried away by her passion. Think for a moment about what makes you feel that passionate, if anything does. Then put one hand over your heart and say, "Great goddess, help me to get in touch with my inner fire and find my way to those things that will warm my spirit. So mote it be."

7. Follow Your Dreams

"We all have dreams. Little wistful longings and big passionate desires. Whether your dreams are about successful careers or enduring love or just having chocolate cake for dessert, simply thinking about them is unlikely to make them happen. It is okay to daydream about things that don't really matter—marrying a prince or becoming a rock star—but if your dreams are important to you, you are going to have to actively pursue them in order to make them come true. Of course, it can be scary to go after your dreams, since you might fail, or they might not live up to your expectations. But if you don't try, you'll never know, will you?"

ACTION: Figure out which one of your dreams is the one you want the most, then take one concrete step toward following that dream.

DIVINATION: This card is a not-so-subtle hint that it is time to stop dreaming and start acting! Or perhaps, if you have taken action already, it is a sign that you are on the right path. You know better than anyone…which do you think it is?

Magic: Sometimes we need an extra little push to get up the courage to follow our dreams. Magical work can give us that. If you have access to a bonfire, light a fire and write your dream down on a piece of paper. Throw the paper into the fire and visualize the sparks flying out into the universe and carrying your dreams with them. Alternatively, if you can't do that, take a votive candle and scratch a word or two describing your dreams into the wax. As it burns down, that will send the energy out in the same way. Open your heart to the possibility of success, knowing that the gods have heard your message.

8. Affirmation for Healing the Heart

"Life can be tough, and there are times when all of us feel sad and broken-hearted. Relationships that don't work out, the loss of pets or human loved ones, illness, disappointments…there are plenty of things that leave us wounded and aching. It is okay to be sad, but when that sadness doesn't go away or interferes with our ability to function in a healthy way, we may need to look outside ourselves for help in moving past it. That can mean family or friends, a counselor, or reaching out to deity for healing. Be kind to yourself and allow others to be kind to you too."

Action: Sometimes the smallest things can be healing to the heart—sitting by the ocean or under the stars, petting an animal, or playing with a child. Doing something nice for someone else. Do one small thing today that puts a smile on your face, or if that is impossible, put a smile on the face of another. Tomorrow, do one more small thing. You might be surprised to see how they add up. (You can even allow someone to do one small kind thing for you.)

Divination: This card may mean you have a heart that is in need of mending. If so, what are you doing to help the process along? Are you doing your best to heal or are you wallowing? If you need help in healing, are you looking for it and accepting it if it is offered? If your heart is doing just fine (and I hope it is), perhaps this card is an indication that you can do something to help someone else whose heart is filled with sorrow. Look around you, and if you see someone who is dealing with heartbreak, reach out and offer a hug or a shoulder to lean on or just an ear to listen.

Magic: If you are stuck in a place of pain and sorrow and having a hard time moving on, try saying this simple affirmation every day for a month (or longer, if it is helping). You can light a candle if you like, or just stand with both hands over your heart and say, "I am broken, but I am healing. My heart grows stronger and more vibrant every day with the love of the god and goddess. I am healing."

9. Give Love

"It is a wonderful thing to be loved. We all want to feel love in our lives—that feeling of warmth and comfort that comes from the knowledge that someone out there is sending love in our direction. But don't forget that love is a street that goes in two directions. As much as you need and want to be loved, others need and want it too. Love is remarkable—the more you give, the more you have to give. If you allow your heart to be filled with love for others, whether that love is romantic or familial, the affection between friends, the love you feel for a beloved animal companion, or even the love for god and goddess, that sense of warmth and joy will overflow like a river. You can give love to those you don't even know; send unconditional love out to the homeless man you pass on the street or the woman who smiles at you in the store. You don't have to say or do anything, necessarily; just open your heart and send love out. Of course, if you are giving love to those you know, you can say it out loud, write it on a card, or just express it with a hug or a kind word. Sometime you will get love back. Sometimes you won't. But that doesn't mean it isn't worth doing."

DIVINATION: This card is telling you to open your heart. Maybe someone has been offering you love but you haven't taken the time and energy to make sure they know you love them too. It is easy to take friends, family, and significant others for granted when your life is hectic, thinking, "Oh, they know I love them," or "I'll do something special later, when I have more time." Perhaps you have been a little self-involved and the gods are gently suggesting that it is time to focus your energies outward instead of inward. It could be that there is someone close to you who is crying out for love, but you just haven't noticed. Look around you. Are you giving enough love to those who are important to you? Life is short and we never know what lies right around the corner. Don't wait until tomorrow to give the love you feel today.

MAGIC: Sit quietly in a dim room or outside under the moon. Light a white or red candle and spend a moment concentrating on its light and warmth. Then close your eyes and feel that light and warmth in the area of your heart. Open yourself to the universal sources of love, god and goddess, or whatever you believe in, and feel your heart filling up with that feeling of warmth and affection. When it fills to the point of overflowing, send that love out into the world. You can direct it at specific people or simply will it to go wherever it is needed most. Spend as long as feels right doing this, then put your hands over your heart and save a little for yourself. Thank the gods for sharing their energy, and blow out the candle.

10. Joy and Delight

"If you look up *joy* in the dictionary, you will find a definition similar to 'a feeling of great happiness or pleasure, especially of an elevated or spiritual kind.' In truth, *joy* means something a little bit different to everyone, but I think we can all agree that it is a rare and wonderful thing. Life is full of sadness and stress, which makes those fleeting moments of joy even more important. One truly joyous memory can get you through a lot of bad days. It doesn't matter how you define joy—what matters is that you seek it out, that you give it every opportunity to enter your life—and that when it does, you make sure to appreciate it to the fullest. If you can do something that brings joy to others, that's a bonus."

ACTION: What brings you joy? Is it spending time with friends or family? Walking in the woods or by the ocean shore alone? Dancing, singing, eating a fresh-baked cookie still hot from the oven? Do you find joy in ritual, communing with the gods? Or playing with children and animals, who are so much better at embracing joy than many adults? Make a list of the ways in which you find joy and try to find time to include at least a few in every week.

DIVINATION: This card has a clear message: find and embrace joy! Maybe you've been feeling down or blue lately or are just too busy being an adult to find the time for life's simple pleasures. Maybe, like so many, you don't feel worthy of joy. If so, I assure you, you are. Either way, if you pulled out this card, you probably need some more joy in your life. It doesn't have to be anything complicated or expensive. You don't have to go to Disney (although hey, if that's where you find your joy, go for it). But you do have to make the effort to seek it out or at the very least create the space and opportunity for joy to come to you. And when it is there, right in front of you, don't shrug it off or be in a hurry to move on to the next thing. Embrace joy fully. Dive into the moment. Yell and grin and leap if that's what's called for. Pretend you're a child and just go with it. Swing higher and kick off your flip flops. Joy is good for the soul. Go find something that brings you joy. Do it now!

MAGIC: Can you do magic for joy? Of course you can. Or at the very least, like doing magic to open yourself to love, you can do magic to open yourself to joy. How many of us miss opportunities for joy just because we aren't paying enough attention or take those rare moments for granted when they do come by? This is a simple spell to invite joy into your life. Find a picture of something that represents joy to you, whether it is the beach at sunset or a day at the Renaissance Faire. If you can't find a picture, it is fine to just make a quick, silly drawing or write it down. Light a red or white candle and say, "God and goddess, please help me to open myself to joy. Remind me of how it feels to embrace those shining moments of pure happiness and send me joy to fill my days and brighten my nights. Help me to bring joy to others as they bring joy to me. So mote it be."

WATER: Change and Movement
1. Healing Waters

"Water has always been associated with healing. There are sacred springs, pools, and wells all over the world. It is traditional in many places to make a pilgrimage to these healing waters, often at the time of the summer solstice, but you can use water for healing work all year round, even if you have to create your own sacred site. (Hint: If you have a bathtub, you're in luck.) Salt and water are often used for cleansing during magical rituals, so if you don't have a body of water nearby, you can still take advantage of Water's healing powers. Or you can just stand outside when it's raining. We're witches; we know how to improvise."

ACTION: Take a healing bath—or a shower if you don't have a tub. Put on some quiet music if you like and add sea salt to the water of the tub or use a salt scrub if you are in the shower. Be mindful of the element of Water as you bathe and visualize illness, pain, and sadness going down the drain. Let the water wash away your troubles like the rain washes dust off a car. Come out of your bath or shower feeling healed and renewed and reconnected with the power of Water.

Divination: This card is a reminder to connect with Water in its most powerful ways. If you can go to a body of water—the ocean, a lake, or even a stream—now is a good time to do so. If you don't have one nearby, maybe buy a small tabletop fountain and spend some time listening to it. The sound of moving water is almost as healing as the waters themselves.

Magic: Make yourself some magical healing water. Fill a clear glass container with water (from a fresh source is great if you can get it, anything from ocean or well water to rainwater you collect, but tap water is fine if that is all you have). If you have a quartz or amethyst crystal (or any other stone associated with healing), put it inside the container. If you want, you can add a sprig of rosemary. Then set the container out in the moonlight for a night or three. If you can't put it outside, place it on a window or table where the moonlight will fall. The full moon is a great time to do this, but if you need it sooner, you don't have to wait. You can then use the water in a bath, to anoint yourself during a healing ritual, or simply wash your face and hands in it while visualizing a glowing, healing light washing you clean.

2. Cleansing Body and Spirit

"As we go through our daily routines, we almost always include some kind of cleaning—baths or showers, washing our faces, brushing our teeth. But it is important to look at cleansing on a level that goes more than skin deep. Body, auras, mind, and spirit all need cleansing from time to time as we walk through a world filled with powerful emotions, chaos, and free floating negativity. Some people also believe that there are dark and unhealthy energies that can attach themselves to the unwary. Either way, it makes sense to occasionally do some cleansing that will wash away the unpleasant, unwanted, and just plain icky stuff we pick up along the way."

ACTION: Basic spiritual cleansing is as simple as being aware that there is a level to cleansing that goes beyond soap and water. Start with mindfulness and the intention to wash away anything negative or harmful and then use whatever form of water suits you best. You can stand under the shower and visualize anything nasty being carried away by the water and flowing down the drain. Or you can stand out in the rain, wade into the ocean, or even take a cloth and dip it in a bowl of water that has been mixed with a little sea salt. The important thing is your focus as you are doing it, rather than how it is done.

DIVINATION: This card is likely telling you that you are carrying around some spiritual or psychic crap you don't need and that getting rid of it will help you get on with the other things you need to do. If you have been feeling dragged down or tired, unusually stressed for no obvious reason, or just plain blue, it may not be normal life stuff. It's possible you simply need a good cleansing, and will feel a lot better afterwards. This card is a suggestion to use the power of Water to do some kind of cleansing.

MAGIC: A magical cleansing bath is a good way to wash yourself clean not only physically, but on a spiritual level as well. Fill a tub with water, and add in some sea salt to help draw out negativity. A few drops of any mild essential oil that is good for cleansing, like rosemary, lemon, or grapefruit, can be added as well. (If you don't have a tub, you can fill a deep bowl and put it in the shower or use it outside where it won't matter if things get wet.) As you sit in the water or splash it over yourself, visualize yourself washing away layers of dark energy, seeing them get lighter and lighter as you go. If you are feeling particularly in need of cleansing, you can ask the gods or the element of Water to help you in the task.

3. Meditation for Peace and Serenity

"In this crazy, hectic world we live in, peace and serenity may be more precious than gold and rarer than the most exotic gemstone. Most of us start running from the moment we get up, fueling ourselves with caffeine so we can keep going when we're exhausted, racing from the demands of work to the demands of home with very little downtime. When we do relax, we often do it in front of some kind of electronic screen—television or computer or phone. Eventually this constant stimulation begins to wear us down, like water on a stone, unless we purposely allow ourselves the occasional break for true peace and serenity."

ACTION: Meditation is a great way to achieve peace and serenity, but if you're not a fan, you can go for a walk (by the ocean or a stream if you are lucky enough to live near one), listen to ocean sounds on a recording while sitting quietly or even sit by an indoor fountain and simply breath while listening to the soothing rhythm of the water. However you choose to do it, giving yourself even fifteen minutes a day to simply do nothing can help you find the energy to do everything life demands of you the rest of the time.

DIVINATION: The card is probably an indication that you are in serious need of some peace and serenity. And maybe a nap. If you have been feeling particularly frazzled and pushed to your limits lately, this card is a reminder to stop for a moment and connect with Water in some way that will help you to relax. You can use some of the suggestions above, do the magical work below, or just stand outside in the rain and let it wash away your troubles. But it is definitely time to make an effort to chill out and take a break.

MAGIC: Sometimes we forget that we can use water in the simplest of ways—by drinking it. If you are in need of some peace and serenity, try making some magical water. Start with a glass of water (the purer the better). You can use a glass jar if you have pets who might get into it and then pour it in a glass later. If you want, you can put a (clean) quartz or amethyst crystal in the bottom and/or a sprig of fresh rosemary or lavender. Leave it out overnight where the moon will shine on it. If you're going to put it outside, definitely use a jar. As you do the preparations, keep in your mind the intention of creating water for use in peace and serenity work. Then, when you use the water the next day, hold it up to the sky and say, "God and goddess, power of Water, please bless and consecrate this water for positive use, that it may bring me peace and serenity with every drop I drink." Then sip it slowly, feeling the calm filling you with every sip.

4. Change and Progress

"Water is all about movement and change. It wears away huge rocks over time to create canyons and carve out the countryside where it runs. Even the calmest lake is always moving, and the ocean waves are in constant flux, ebbing and flowing with the tides. We can tap into the power of Water to help us with our own movement, using its energy to help us make positive changes in our lives and move forward towards whatever is next on our paths."

ACTION: Change can be frightening, but there is no progress without change. Think about the Nile river in Egypt. Every year it flooded, which seems destructive. But those very floods were what nourished the soil, making the lands of the Nile valley among the most fertile in the world, and allowing them to build an amazing civilization. Use the flood times in your own life—the times of trouble that seem out of your control—to push you in the direction of positive change. But also remember that water can be directed, and make sure that your energy is taking you where you want to go.

DIVINATION: Not unlike the Tower card in the tarot, this card may be an indication that your life is in a time of change and flux, not necessarily in ways that are all that pleasant when you are living through them. But remember that when things fall apart, it gives you the opportunity to rebuild them in ways that are more productive and positive. Or maybe you are finally achieving those things you have worked toward for a long time and making serious progress toward your goals. In which case, hurrah, and keep going!

MAGIC: There is a simple way to do magical work for change and progress and all you need are two glasses and some water. You can put them on your altar or anywhere they won't be disturbed. Start with all the water in the glass on the left and the one on the right empty. Each day for a week (or longer—you can even do this a little bit at a time following the changes of the moon, starting with the dark moon and ending up on the night of the full moon)—pour a little bit of the water from the glass on the left into the one on the right. Say, "I am moving in the direction of positive change and progress." Really feel the energy of change being boosted by the power of the element of Water. When all the water is in the glass on the right, take that energy and do something to create positive change in your life.

5. Water Magic

"Water is a powerful force. It can wear down a mountain or create a lake. It brings life to the fields, but can also be violent and impossible to control. Not an element to be taken for granted, as you will know if you have ever been thirsty or lived through either a drought or a flood. Most of the time, though, Water is our friend, and we can use its power to help us change and transition through various stages of our lives. Water is fluid and flexible, and reminds us that we can be that way too."

ACTION: To connect with the magic of Water, take a few minutes to immerse yourself in it. If you live near a lake or stream or ocean, go sit in the water, or at the water's edge with at least your feet submerged, and really pay attention. Listen to its voice, watch its movement, follow its path. There is magic in all of those things. If you don't have a body of water nearby, go out in the rain or sit in the tub or take a shower whose purpose is more about connection and less about getting clean in a hurry. Feel the flow moving over you and think about the fact that a large part of the human body is made up of water, so the Water is always a part of us.

DIVINATION: This card is telling you to make a magical connection to Water. You can do it by following the exercise above or doing anything else that makes you feel the element of Water in its more-than-mundane form. Even drinking a glass of water can be magical if you focus on sensing the molecules being absorbed by your body and becoming a part of your own essence. Remember that the element of Water can take many shapes: freshwater and saltwater; rain, snow, fog, sleet, or ice; forceful or gentle; wild and natural or tamed by man. Take a day or a week to connect with it in as many different forms as you can and thank each one for the gift it brings.

MAGIC: To make a magical connection to Water, fill a bowl with the freshest water you can find. (You can collect rainwater if you don't have a well or live by a natural source, but tap water is fine if that's all you have.) If you can do this on the night of the full moon, that's a bonus, although it isn't necessary. Think about how the moon affects the tides, the water ebbing and flowing due to forces beyond its control. Our lives are much the same, aren't they? Maybe that is because so much of the human body is made up of water. Think of all the ways in which water is so necessary to our existence. Place your fingers in the bowl and swirl them around as you list the various benefits of water: drinking, bathing, cooking, flushing toilets! Then say thank you to the power of Water, touching your wet fingers to your third eye (the center of your forehead), your lips, your heart, your core (near your belly button). Place your hands back in the water and spend a moment letting that gratitude resonate through your whole body. When you're done, you can use the water on your plants or put some aside for magical work later.

6. Make a Move

"It is important to keep moving. This is true in the literal sense because the body functions best when it gets a certain amount of exercise, and it is true in the metaphorical sense. If we don't keep moving forward in our lives, our only other choices are to go backward—rarely a good idea—or to stay still, which may work for a while, but is no more healthy for the spirit than staying still all the time is healthy for the body. As witches, our goal is to become the best human beings (and witches) we can be. That means continuing to grow and change and learn—and *that* means moving forward. Even if it is just a little bit at a time."

ACTION: Water is all about change and movement. The only water that isn't moving is stagnant, and usually that's a bad thing, both for the water and for everything that depends on it. Make sure you aren't just sitting still. Get up and do some form of exercise today, whether it is walking, biking, dancing, or even cleaning the house (yes, that counts). Then think about your goals and aspirations and do one thing, no matter how small, that moves you closer to achieving them.

DIVINATION: This card is probably a not-so-subtle hint to get off your butt. Have you been spending a lot of time sitting in one place, maybe in front of the TV or the computer? GET UP. Move around, do something, accomplish a task, any task. Or maybe the issue is deeper than just daily inertia. Are you actively working on creating positive change and forward movement in your life? If not, this card is undoubtedly the universe telling you to stop stalling and just DO IT. Not tomorrow. Not next week. Now. Today. Make a move!

MAGIC: If you want to move forward but are feeling stuck, don't worry. It happens to all of us from time to time. Use the power of Water to help you get moving again. Fill a shallow bowl halfway with water. Light a blue or white candle and face the west if you can. This is a good one to do on the full moon, if the timing works out, but you can always visualize the moonlight shining on the water, if you can't have the real thing, or use the light from the candle to substitute for it. Gaze at the light on the water and think about how the moon goes through its changing phases every month, from dark to full and back again to dark, waxing and waning with the rhythm of the universe. Then think about your life and what you want to achieve. Put your fingers lightly into the water and swirl it around in a clockwise direction. Say, "Power of Water, help me to become less stuck and more fluid. Help me to grow in energy every day, moving purposely toward my goals, drawing on your power and the power of the moon. Help me to move forward in any and all positive ways. So mote it be." Then flick the water on your fingers in the general direction of the moon and gaze at the movement of the water in the bowl until you are ready to rejoin the world.

7. Go with the Flow

"Most of us spend a lot of time fighting the challenges and obstacles life puts in our way or pushing back against aspects of our reality we don't like. That's not a bad thing, in and of itself, and many times it is necessary. The trick is in knowing when to fight, when that resistance is only going to frustrate us and sap our energy, and when to go with the flow instead. Sometimes (to paraphrase some other folks) you just have to give in and give goddess. In short, acknowledge that there is nothing you can do, make your peace with the situation the best you can, and have faith that the gods will make everything work out in the end (even if the way it works out doesn't necessarily make sense to you at the time)."

ACTION: Do something that is easy and fun. Put your problems and concerns aside for the moment and just live, even if it is only for a few hours. Have a relaxed meal with family or friends. Take a dog for a walk (dogs are great at going with the flow).

Float in a pool or the ocean or a tub. Take a little space of time to allow yourself to just *be*.

DIVINATION: If there is something in your life that you're using a lot of time, energy, and spirit to fight, this card may be a sign that it is time to stop, at least for a while. Is there a different way of approaching the issue, maybe one that involves compromise or less effort? Can you back away and just let it be for a while? Sometimes going with the flow for a day or two helps you find your way to letting go for good.

MAGIC: Using a source of moving water (a stream or river, rain, or even the water coming from your faucet or some that you pour from a pitcher), picture a goal in your mind and then infuse it into the water. Feel your intentions moving out into the world as the water flows. Then let go and allow the intentions to blossom into fruition if they're going to.

8. Affirmation for Positive Change

"Change can be scary, and sometimes we resist making changes because we are afraid we will make things worse instead of better. The best way to get past this fear is to direct your energy toward making sure any shifts are positive. Ask the power of Water to move you in the right direction and put out your intention into the world as clearly and decisively as you can."

ACTION: It seems like a simple thing, but doing one small act each day toward whatever positive changes you wish to achieve will eventually move you closer to your goal. If every day you pull a few weeds, eventually you will have a neater garden. Need to have more money? Start by saving the change from your pockets and putting it into a jar every day. Want more love in your life? Put a little bit out into the universe every day, even if it seems as though you aren't getting anything back. Want to run a 5K? Start by walking around the block. Every act that moves you forward, no matter how small, not only gets you closer to your goal, but reinforces your message to the universe that this is what you really want.

DIVINATION: This card may be a hint that you need to have more faith in yourself and your ability to achieve your goals. Or maybe a reminder that positive change is as much about the journey as it is the place you end up. Keep putting one foot in front of the other, and focus on what you want to achieve. You can do it!

Magic: To help achieve positive change, light a blue or white candle and say this affirmation. (If things don't seem to be moving forward, try saying it every day, with or without the candle.) "I am strong and capable, and every day moves me closer to achieving the positive changes I desire."

9. Tears of Joy and Sadness

"Life is rarely simple. There is no such thing as completely good or bad; even the best outcomes may come with a price, and even the worst disasters can often have a silver lining. Loss and grief show us the value of what we had, and how lucky we were to have it. The toughest challenges give us the opportunity to rise above. That doesn't mean that the hard stuff isn't *hard*. Of course it is. But if you can find the positive side of even the worst events, it will help you to stay strong and keep moving forward. Maybe you can even inspire others who are dealing with their own difficulties to keep moving forward too."

Action: Think about the tough times you have come through in the past and look back at what followed. Did you survive? Did you grow from the experiences and become stronger or wiser or kinder? Did a closing door open another one for something good? If so, take a deep breath, look at whatever you're dealing with right now (and let's face it, most of us are dealing with something), and remind yourself that one way or the other, it is going to work out okay. Perhaps not the way you want it to, but okay.

DIVINATION: This card may be an indication that you are struggling with tough times. Or perhaps you are coming out the other side. Maybe both. Either way, stay strong and smile when you can, even if it is through your tears. If this card doesn't represent you, perhaps it is a reminder that even those who present a happy face to the world may be hiding tears underneath. Be kind and give people the benefit of the doubt. You never know what they are dealing with behind closed doors.

MAGIC: It's okay to be sad. It is also okay to be happy, even when things are horrible. There are two sides to every coin, and no situation is black and white. Getting through day-to-day life is often dependent on finding a balance. In a quiet or sacred space, place two glasses or goblets of water in front of you, one almost full, the other almost empty. Say, "God and goddess, please help me to find and keep my balance in this challenging world." Pour water from the fuller glass into the emptier one until they are as close to even as you can get them. Then pour a little back. Do this a few times, and when you feel that you have a sense of balance, sip a little from each glass and raise them each to the gods in thanks.

10. Rebirth and Reinvention

"We are all born, and some day we will all die. Along the way, we recreate ourselves—either intentionally or through circumstances beyond our control—becoming far different from the children, teens, or young adults we once were. For many of us, finding a new spiritual faith is a kind of rebirth. For some, it is the discovery or acceptance of a different sexuality or gender identity, a change in careers, finding or losing love, becoming a parent, or losing your own. For women, menopause often causes a huge shift in how we see ourselves, and retirement can do that too. Embrace each life-shaking change as it happens, as frightening or unsettling as it may be, and rejoice in your rebirth as a new person, with a fresh path before you."

ACTION: Think about all the major shifts your life has taken over the years and how you have changed from where you started out because of them. Are you happy with the person you are now? Put a candle in a cupcake and celebrate who you turned out to be. If you're not happy with the person you are now, put that candle in a cupcake anyway...but when you light it, vow to rebirth yourself and become your best possible you.

DIVINATION: This card is indicating one of two things. Either you are in the midst of or just coming out of a big shift, in which case it is time to celebrate your rebirth, or you are overdue to reinvent yourself, and this card is a push in that direction. Have you been wavering on the cusp of making a substantive change? This card may be telling you it is time to go for it!

MAGIC: If you want to celebrate some form of rebirth in your life, here is a simple magical ceremony. Using either a bath or shower (or even a large bucket or bowl of water outside, if you have the privacy to do so, or a lake or stream, if you are lucky enough to have one nearby), prepare for a transition ritual. Burn some sage if you like or float a few herbs or flowers on the water. Find a robe or comfortable clothes to put on afterward. These will symbolize your new self, so they should be both comfortable and if possible, very different from whatever clothes you normally wear. Take off your clothes slowly and mindfully, as if you were shedding your old skin. Step into the water and submerge yourself or splash the water over yourself from head to foot. Close your eyes and envision yourself inside an egg, cracking it open, and coming out fresh and new. Feel the water washing away your old self, and when you are ready, get out, dry yourself off, and put on your different clothes. *Really feel* how deep the changes have gone, and know that from this moment forward, you will never be the exact same person you were.

Chapter Six

How to Use this Deck with the Everyday Witch Tarot

Naturally, this oracle deck can be used completely on its own. But some people will want to occasionally combine its use with its companion deck, the Everyday Witch Tarot. There are a couple of different ways you can do that.

1. Do a regular tarot spread and then use a card from the oracle deck to clarify the reading.
2. Pull one card from each deck and see if there is a unifying message when you put them together.
3. Pull one to three cards from each deck every day for a week or a month, and write down which

cards you are getting. See if there are any consistent repeats or ways in which the messages from one deck support or reinforce the message from the other. (In which case, you should probably be paying attention to whatever message they are trying to give you.)

4. If you are trying to work on some particular goal, you can pull a card or cards from each deck that symbolize that goal and place them on your altar or someplace else where you will see them regularly (like your bathroom mirror or the front of the refrigerator) to remind you of that goal.

5. Use a card or cards from each deck together to empower your magical work.

6. Any other way that suits you!

To Write to the Author

If you wish to contact the author or would like more information about this book, please write to the author in care of Llewellyn Worldwide Ltd. and we will forward your request. Both the author and publisher appreciate hearing from you and learning of your enjoyment of this book and how it has helped you. Llewellyn Worldwide Ltd. cannot guarantee that every letter written to the author can be answered, but all will be forwarded. Please write to:

Deborah Blake
c/o Llewellyn Worldwide
2143 Wooddale Drive
Woodbury, MN 55125-2989

Please enclose a self-addressed stamped envelope for reply, or $1.00 to cover costs. If outside the U.S.A., enclose an international postal reply coupon.

Many of Llewellyn's authors have websites with additional information and resources.
For more information, please visit our website at
http://www.llewellyn.com